You must remember that I have a dual personality. One
is a brave Indian and the other is a sensitive animal.
                                    —Paul Gauguin

Gauguin's art might bring visions of bright sunlight,

colourful flowers and beautiful, tropical women. It is

not difficult for us to appreciate the wild passion and

personality expressed in his artwork, but it is hard to

comprehend just why this extraordinary man aban-

doned his family and life as a stockbroker in Paris

for the exotic shores of the Pacific island, Tahiti.

This book opens the door to Gauguin's life, inner world

and imagination. It reveals the fascinating contradictions

of character that influenced his art.

Mason Crest
450 Parkway Drive, Suite D
Broomall, PA 19008
www.masoncrest.com

Printed and bound in the United States of America.

First printing
9 8 7 6 5 4 3 2 1

Series ISBN: 978-1-4222-2839-5
ISBN: 978-1-4222-2854-8
ebook ISBN: 978-1-4222-8974-7

The Library of Congress has cataloged the
        hardcopy format(s) as follows:

        Library of Congress Cataloging-in-Publication Data

Cook, Diane.
  [Paul Gauguin]
  Paul Gauguin : 19th-century French painter / Diane Cook.
      pages cm. — (People of importance)
  ISBN 978-1-4222-2854-8 (hardcover) — ISBN 978-1-4222-2839-5 (series) — ISBN 978-1-4222-8974-7 (ebook)
  1. Gauguin, Paul, 1848-1903—Juvenile literature. 2. Painters—France—Biography—Juvenile literature. I. Title.
  ND553.G27C64 2014
  759.4—dc23
  [B]
                                        2013008220

Produced by Vestal Creative Services.
www.vestalcreative.com
Illustrations copyright © 2001 Yan Thomas.

People of Importance

PAUL GAUGUIN: 19th-Century French Painter

Diane Cook   Yan Thomas

Mason Crest

ALINE'S WORDS

This morning, Mother got a letter from Father. Today is 3 January, 1897, and the letter is dated 18 September, 1896. So it took three and a half months to travel from Tahiti, across the Pacific Ocean to here, in Denmark. At the end of the letter, Father wrote, "I send the boys and Aline, my dear daughter, a big, big hug. It has been such a long time since I last saw them."

I held my father's letter to my face, breathed in the sugary smell of exotic fruits—coconut, banana, mango—and cried.

I don't know my father well. When I was a little girl, he told us stories of travels in faraway mysterious lands. But since he left ten years ago, I've only seen him twice.

Ten days ago, I turned 20. I wish he were here. I know he is sick and weak. Mother says it is silly of me to worry about him, that he is the one to blame and he shouldn't have left his family behind.

When I was ten I resented the absence of my father. It hurt to think how selfishly he left us, becoming a stranger to his family. And all for what? To make paintings that did not sell and were judged second rate at best. But as I grew up I realised it was not all that simple.

I had a privileged life as a young child. We had lots of toys and dolls and puppets and also a pet cat. On Sundays, we would go for joyful walks in the park and Father would push us on the swings or take his drawing pencils out and sketch us.

One day, a visiting card was left on a table. I read it: *Paul Gauguin, Stockbroker*. Mother explained that Father was working in a bank and that he was in charge of investing money at the stock exchange. She was obviously proud of him.

One morning Father said, "I quit my job last night. It is all over. I'll never go back to my office." I felt surprised. "But, Father, what are you going to do?"

"I will paint," he answered. "I will make paintings every day. It's more interesting than watching over every piece of iron, coal and sugar, don't you think?"

At that point, Mother flared up and they quarrelled fiercely. I could hear Mother shouting, "Why can't you feel happy with being an amateur painter? I know the ones to blame: your artist friends. They are manipulating you, the so-called 'Impressionists.' All of them are lazy bohemians! Do you expect them to pay for your rent or even lend you money?"

I was flabbergasted. I rushed to my room and locked myself in. Father quietly opened the door of my room and sat at the end of the bed. He kept silent for a minute and then said, "Don't worry, Aline. We all love each other. We'll find a solution."

Then he started talking about himself and his childhood in Peru. He told his story with great passion. He had to come back to Paris for school at the age of seven and this upset him. As soon as he finished school, he joined a ship and travelled around the world.

Suddenly, he stood up and took off the lid of a shoebox he had brought in with him. He showed me the pictures inside. There were masks of African sorcerers, heads of Egyptian mummies, and stone Buddhas from India. This was a collection of his favourite primitive art. To be honest, I felt rather pleased that my father loved art so much. I enjoyed watching him sitting at his easel in his studio.

Sometimes he would lend me pastels to draw. When I tried to draw a little dog but felt disappointed by my results, I would say, "This is all wrong. It does not look like a dog!" He would answer, "Don't say that! It looks quite lovely to me. Likeness does not matter!"

Mother packed all our belongings and took us to the railway station, where we got on a train to Copenhagen, Mother's hometown where Grandmother lived. "Isn't Father coming along?" I asked, knowing the answer.

One night, I heard low voices in the kitchen. I quitely tiptoed onto the landing. Mother and Grandmother were talking in the kitchen.

"Mette, my daughter, don't worry. I will take care of you and the children, since your husband won't do it. How disgraceful! Giving up his job to become an artist when you have a family to maintain! He's a fool! My poor darling, you married the wrong man!"

Last month, while sorting through boxes in the attic, I came across on old issue of a French newspaper dated January 1882. On the front page, a title was printed in capital letters, "STOCK-EXCHANGE CRISIS—Bankruptcy of General Union Causes Exchange Crisis." I was not sure what it meant, so I showed it to my French teacher. She explained that in such a crisis, money becomes valueless and people who had savings in a bank lose everything.

All of a sudden, I understood: Father did not leave his position at the bank on a whim. He was dismissed. He was too proud and did not want Mother and his in-laws in Copenhagen to know the truth. Mother and Grandmother thought he had given up everything, so they looked down on him. In fact, he had no choice. How unhappy he must have been!

My younger brother Clovis told me that Father went through a lot of trouble to find a new job. He even posted notices on walls in railway stations.

Clovis was the only one of us to stay with Father in Paris. Having one of his children next to him was a real comfort for Father. But one winter Clovis caught the flu. Father wrote to us and Mother became worried. She thought Father was unable to look after a sick child.

She got on the first train to Paris and brought Clovis back, leaving Father all alone from then on. Mother also brought back several of Father's paintings. I thought she would hang them on the wall, but she locked them up.

One of the paintings I liked very much because it was a portrait of Clovis and my sister with a sleeping kitten. Every time Mother went out on an errand, I would open the cupboard and secretly look at the painting. One day the painting was gone. I waited for Mother to come back to ask her why. She looked at me sadly and said, "I had to sell it." Then she added, "You know, you father is only happy if his paintings sell."

After some time alone in Paris, Father became hungry with no money to live on. He decided it was time to leave. One day we received a postcard from Brittany. In the picture, you can see ladies in strange costumes, wearing white lace headdresses and black clogs.

Father had settled in Pont Aven, a tiny village where many unknown poor painters had gathered. Away from the material comforts of Paris, they could get bed and breakfast there for less than three French francs.

The other artists were impressed with his new, simplistic style. They elected him their leader.

Father knew an art gallery in Paris kept by Mr. Theo van Gogh, who sold one of his paintings. Father sent half of the money from the sale to Mother, and he used the rest to travel, joining Vincent van Gogh, Theo's brother. Vincent was also an unsuccessful painter, just like Father. He lived in Arles, Provence.

At the beginning, Father was happy to be with his friend. They would go together for walks in the countryside and look for a good spot to do some painting. But eventually things went wrong between them, and whenever they talked about painting, they disagreed. I could imagine them talking.

"To paint this, you should keep close to what your eyes can see." That's what Vincent must have said. And Father would say, "Absolutely not. The brush strokes must be large and smooth. The painter shouldn't imitate nature. He should trust his fancy."

Father, who is rather rough tempered, probably lost his self-control. As for Vincent, he was prone to fits of madness. One night, he suddenly jumped at Father with a razor in his hand. As he was about to cut Father, he suddenly stopped, turned around, ran to his room and cut off his own ear.

The police were called and Vincent was taken to a hospital. My father left Arles the day after. I think poor Mr. van Gogh wounded himself willingly to punish himself for almost hurting Father.

Back in Paris, my father was a famous painter. Yet, he did not sell many paintings. Those he did sell were always at a low price. But he made enough of a living to visit us in Copenhagen. How happy we all were, after being separated for five years.

When he visited, we took daily walks together. I liked to hold his arm. I thought it would be nice if his visits went on forever. One day, he said he was going to leave soon and go very far away, to the other end of the world.

He told everybody in Paris that he was going to leave, but no one believed him. Father was not the first to have uttered such words, but few had actually left. He said that he planned to create a "Tropical Workshop," become an artist of the Polynesian Islands and live like a native.

When he said that, his friends did not take him seriously. "Leave? Where to? He doesn't even know! He will never leave." And then one day, in April 1891, he announced he would be departing the following day.

The voyage lasted more than a month. What was going on in his mind all the time? Was he thinking of the sunny island he was going to discover, a sort of earthly paradise with its shimmering white sandy beaches? Was he thinking of me too?

When Father disembarked in Tahiti, the natives warmly welcomed him. The women wove crowns and collars out of bright flowers and offered them to him.

Nature was so generous in Tahiti that you only needed to lift your hand to pick fruit, and bend down to a freshwater spring to quench your thirst. Singing, playing and dancing made the time fly there. Huts were left with doors open, and there were neither robberies nor crimes. And we called them savages?

O.REDON

E.BERNARD

T.LAUTREC

DEGAS

Father settled in a wood hut in the middle of the coconut trees, not far from the seaside. He led the life of a native with few clothes and bare feet. In no time he got used to walking on sand and stones. Father started making lots of pencil drawings in order to soak in the atmosphere. He always appreciated the people's attitudes and gestures, all so natural and spontaneous.

The men and women dressed in brightly coloured *pareos*, or wraparound skirts, usually made from a rectangular piece of printed cloth with large flower designs—colourful and beautiful in the sunlight of the southern tropics.

A year later, Father took up his brushes. He wanted to paint a portrait of a Tahitian girl who lived near him. One morning as she timidly looked into the hut of the strange European, Father asked her to sit for him. She grinned and ran away. "What a pity!" Father thought to himself. But that very afternoon, she returned wearing a large smile. She had put on her finest dress!

Not only did Father carefully watch the Polynesian people and landscape, he also constantly remembered the artwork of other cultures, whether Asian, European or American. Because he feared he might forget, he took along the old shoebox he had shown me in Copenhagen.

This box was his personal portable museum. "I am packing up companions I can talk to everyday," he told me.

What sort of company were those mementos in a box? Ceramics from his native place, potteries from Peru, Egyptian wall paintings from the tombs of the Pharaohs—all of them were ancient pieces from lost civilisations that touched his wild soul deeply. These were works that Europeans considered primitive, gross, awkward and childish.

Father even tried his hand at these ancient techniques, however unsophisticated and rough: oven-heated ceramics, wood engravings and wood sculptures. For him, all techniques were equally worthwhile as long as they expressed the vision and feelings of the artist. Art is everywhere, not only in museums.

Gradually, Father lost his illusions. He realised that the golden age of the Oceanic civilisation belonged to the past. Polynesia was a victim of

modern times—what the settlers and
missionaries called progress. The local
traditions had disappeared, slowly pushed
off by both fashions and culture coming
from Europe. The Island lifestyle gave way
to a growing emphasis on trade and business.
Their new religion was work and profit.
The day when natives robbed his hut,
Father did not feel revengeful. He
understood his burglars had been spoiled
by the Western values of owning and
consuming.

One day when Father went for a swim in the ocean outside his hut, a couple of policemen ordered him to get out of the water because he had been swimming naked. Father thought it very strange. He wondered when the people of Tahiti started using bathing suits!

Meanwhile, his exhibitions were in France. When Father became ill, he thought he might as well sail back to Paris, to take care of his health and then promote his career. He imagined his former friends rushing to welcome him and say, "Hi, Paul, tell us everything about life there!" He was not only proud, but he was also a little vain. After all, not everyone had the courage to leave everything behind to go live on an island in the South Pacific!

However, when he arrived in Paris, Father realised that many of his former acquaintances had forgotten him after all the years of separation. They considered him an odd character—just as the natives and settlers in Tahiti did when he first arrived there.

Worse, in Paris, the capital of modern art, fashions come and go. Father had been celebrated when he was in Brittany as the painter from Pont Aven. But now he was viewed as an old master, out of touch. The young generation of painters was looking somewhere else.

Father sold his last paintings in Paris, but he was a failure. "Do you want to entertain your children?" one newspaper wrote. "Send them to the Gauguin exhibition. They will have fun looking at coloured pictures of female monkeys."

Father was even forced to buy back the paintings that did not sell. When the exhibition closed down, he cried like a child.

When he returned to Tahiti, he was appalled at how much the island had changed. Electric street lamps now lit the lanes. Modern conveniences, all fashionable in Paris, like the phonograph, for example, were all over Tahiti.

"Why go so far if I have to see what I was running away from?" he thought. Shutting himself up in his hut, Father tried to concentrate on the ancient Maori legends.

This morning, Mother handed an envelope to me. I was surprised because I don't often get mail. Father was writing personally to me. I ran to my room and tore open the envelope.

"Dear Aline, you are so big now. But you have not really changed. If I could, I would soon send you

nice presents to decorate
your Christmas tree."

The present I would like
best is a visit from Father, even
for just a couple of days.

PAUL GAUGUIN'S WORDS

One day I woke up earlier than
usual and decided to go to Papeete to fetch
my mail. I had been waiting in vain for
four months and got nothing. Would
there be anything today?

There was a letter. How excited I felt! I recognised Mette's handwriting without having to check the Copenhagen postage stamp.

The letter contained five lines, not more, to let me know the news. My hand started trembling, the letter fell to the ground. I could not speak.

Aline, my daughter, had died from pneumonia, after catching cold. Oh Aline, don't you know how cold the January nights in Denmark can be? Why didn't you wrap up better?

Ever since childhood, misfortune has been roaming around me. It seemed as though an enemy was up there taking me as a constant target.

I felt utterly discouraged. I came straight home, looked for a trunk under my bed and took out my notebook for Aline, which I had meant to be hers after my death. I opened it and read what I had written five years earlier. "To my daughter, I dedicate this notebook. These thoughts are a reflection of my deepest self. She, like me, is wild and she will understand these lines. A young man who is unable to act will age before his time."

I had been a total failure. Who was I? Exhausted, discouraged, sick and old, I felt deeply wounded. I had lost my appetite and my ability to sleep. I made up my mind to do away with it all.

One evening, I swallowed the contents of a bottle of poison. I went to the heart of the forest to lie down. But I took too much of the poison and spit it out. All I got was nausea and a terrible stomach cramp.

I then started the large painting that was to be my last, the summing up of all my art, titled *Where are we from? Who are we? Where are we going?*

I became totally engrossed in painting, banishing all other care or thought. I worked at the 4-metre (13-foot) long canvas day and night for a whole month, putting all my strength into it. All I

wanted was to say what I thought about humanity's origin and fate. I wanted to tell my desire to regain what I had once possessed, and then lost—purity, the soul of a child, the soul of a native.

In 1901, a new century began, the 20th. Everybody was looking toward the future, but I kept looking back. Tahiti had become contaminated by Western civilisation, so I made up my mind to leave this island for another located 1500 kilometres (930 miles) further northeast, in the archipelago of the Marquise Islands. It was Hiva Hoa, called Dominique by the settlers.

Some people tried to talk me out of going there, because the natives were cannibals. I was told that missionaries had been eaten up not so long ago. But that was precisely what I was looking for, a wild country yet untouched by modern civilisation.

When the ship reached the coast, I set foot on the beach, and the curious natives came near. I admit that I felt rather scared, especially when I saw a woman's naked body completely covered with extraordinary tattooing. But, in a short time, they were calling me "Koke" which means "the image maker."

I spent a month building my wooden hut and sculpting my door. Then I planted coconut trees and vanilla trees. I kept on sculpting and painting, but little by little I felt my strength going. I was hardly strong enough to feed myself. I lay down for hours on end, unable to move. I closed my eyes and thought, "What did I expect from life?" I had only wanted one thing—to have my own way.

BIOGRAPHY

Author Diane Cook is a journalist and freelance writer. She has written hundreds of newspaper articles and writes regularly for national magazines, trade publications and websites. She lives in Dover, Delaware, with her husband and three children.